Thuy Nguyen

Code Switching

A sociolinguistic perspective

Anchor Compact

Nguyen, Thuy: Code Switching: A sociolinguistic perspective. Hamburg, Anchor Academic Publishing 2014
Original title of the thesis: The Sociolinguistic Dimension of Code Switching

Buch-ISBN: 978-3-95489-270-9
PDF-eBook-ISBN: 978-3-95489-770-4
Druck/Herstellung: Anchor Academic Publishing, Hamburg, 2014

Bibliografische Information der Deutschen Nationalbibliothek:
Die Deutsche Nationalbibliothek verzeichnet diese Publikation in der Deutschen Nationalbibliografie; detaillierte bibliografische Daten sind im Internet über http://dnb.d-nb.de abrufbar.

Bibliographical Information of the German National Library:
The German National Library lists this publication in the German National Bibliography. Detailed bibliographic data can be found at: http://dnb.d-nb.de

© Anchor Academic Publishing, ein Imprint der Diplomica® Verlag GmbH
http://www.diplom.de, Hamburg 2014
Printed in Germany

1. Introduction

According to the World Atlas of Language Structure there are nearly seven thousand languages spoken throughout the world and more than half of the worlds' population is estimated to be bilingual and engages in code switching. Due to such statistics it becomes obvious that nowadays the alternation between two languages is rather the norm than exception in many communities. However, the fact that bilingualism is so widespread is not the only reason why there has been and still is such an interest in this phenomenon as a research topic. The question arises why the study of language behaviour over and over remains an interesting subject in linguistic research.

A probable answer might be that language with all its features is not a static but a dynamic concept and has always been subject to political, social as well as economic changes throughout human history. Accordingly, a phenomenon such as bilingualism is above all the result of historical progresses. But not only languages underlie everlasting changes, it is also the perception of different languages and the attitudes towards them that have changed. The fact that individuals are capable of speaking more than one language has nowadays been widely accepted and is even promoted since bilingualism has proved to be rather an advantage than a drawback.

Code switching, the alternative use of two languages within the same conversation, remains one of the central issues in bilingualism research. For a long time, code switching has been considered as a lack of linguistic competence since it was taken as evidence that bilinguals are not able to acquire two languages or keep them apart properly. Thus, it was regarded as result of not knowing at least one of the languages very well. Consequently, there was a lack of interest in studying this phenomenon until the 1970ies. Since then linguists began to deal with the subject in considerable detail. Nowadays it is the common belief that code switching is grammatically structured and systematic and therefore can no longer be regarded as deficient language behaviour.

The purpose of this essay is to explore the question why bilingual speakers engage in code switching based on selected theories. In the course of research code switching has been studied from different perspectives. On the one hand, code switching has been dealt with from a grammatical perspective. Approaches under this perspective aim at identifying grammatical constraints that underlie code switching. However, although a grammatical point remains important it fails to answer the question of why switching occurs. An exclusively grammatical perspective is therefore not sufficient to describe the reasons for an effect of a switch. Therefore I want to deal with code switching from a sociolinguistic point of view which looks beyond the formal aspects and concentrates on the social, pragmatic and cultural functions that code switching may have.

The starting point in the sociolinguistic study of code switching is to recognize that the choice of a particular language is not a random behaviour and may even be predictable. Being aware of this fact, the central question comes up why bilinguals use different language varieties in the same utterance. Does a switch between languages carry any specific social meaning at all? Based on this question, sociolinguistic research further explores the question in which situations code switching is probable and which functions it may serve for the individual speaker.

The second chapter begins with a description and definition of the terms monolingualism, bilingualism and multilingualism which are relevant for understanding code switching since this phenomenon cannot be regarded as an isolated phenomenon. Code switching is a central part of the bilingual discourse.

The third chapter deals with a detailed description and definition of the term code switching. First of all, code switching is categorized and classified as a language contact phenomenon. Moreover, defining code switching includes distinguishing the term from other language contact phenomena such as borrowing. The chapter further continues with the definition of code switching. In order to demonstrate how the perception of code switching has changed throughout the course of research history, several definitions will be considered which reveal the different viewpoints on the subject. Finally, this chapter is closed with a distinction between three different types of code switching that may occur in bilingual speech. The following part gives an overview of selected sociolinguistic theories which are an attempt to explain the circumstances under which code switching occurs and the motivations speakers have when choosing another language within the same conversation. In general, one can roughly distinguish between macro level approaches and micro level approaches in sociolinguistics. Macro-level approaches take situational factors and above all societal norms and structures into account when explaining individual speech behaviour. This approach explores language choices at a community level.

Joshua Fishman's domain analysis serves an appropriate example of an approach applying a macro-level perspective. It has set an important milestone in sociolinguistic research focussing on the relationship between language and society and more precisely on the relationship between language choices and certain types of activity. The assumption is that language choices become predictable on the basis of the domain in which they occur.

In contrast to that, micro level approaches regard the motivations for code switching not deriving from overall societal norms but from the interlocutors themselves. With micro-level approaches, code switching is explored at an interactional level.

Jan Blom and John J. Gumperz were the first to concentrate on the functions of code switching for the discourse itself and later on introduced the term conversational code switching. Code switching is, according to Gumperz, regarded as a contextualization cue which speakers strategically use to mark their speech. Gumperz's work proved to be very influential for the ongoing research on code switching.

It is especially Peter Auer's work which can be understood as a detailed reflexion and modification of Gumperz's theory of conversational code switching. Auer proposes the method of conversation analysis which is a detailed transcription of speech exchanges between interlocutors within a conversation in order to get to an interpretation of the meaning conveyed by code switching.

With a particular focus on the psychological forces underlying language behaviour, speech accommodation theory set up by Howard Giles and his colleagues serves as an attempt to explain languages choices in terms of convergence and divergence. Thus, speakers adjust their speech style as a way of expressing certain attitudes and intentions towards the interlocutor.

Carol Myers–Scotton is also interested in identifying the psychological and social motivations underlying code switching and introduces the markedness model. According to this model code switching is regarded as the negotiation of the relationships between speakers. Moreover, the markedness model is an effort to combine the study on code switching at a micro – and macro-level since she uses the conversation between bilinguals as unit of analysis but also considers social norms and expectations as influencing factors.

The following chapter includes a detailed discussion of these approaches mentioned above with the purpose to compare and evaluate them. In doing this, I concentrate on the following questions:

· What do these approaches have in common?
· What are the main differences between these approaches?
· To what extent have these approaches contributed to the understanding of code switching and its social meaning?
· In which points are these approaches limited and disputable?

The last chapter in this critical essay includes a summary of the most important aspects which have been discussed here. Finally, I will close this chapter by drawing a conclusion on/about the importance of the discussed approaches for the prospective research of code switching.

2. Terminology and definitions

2.1 Monolingualism

Monolingualism or unilingualism describes the condition of an individual or a community having access to only one linguistic code and therefore speaking only one language. This usually refers to the language which is acquired as a first language or mother tongue. Besides, the term is sometimes used to refer to a language policy which enforces one official or national language over others. Although monolingualism had been so far and is in some communities still regarded as the norm, there are less monolingual people or groups than there are bilinguals or multilinguals within the world population nowadays.

On the one hand, monolingualism is likely to occur in isolated tribes and on the other hand particularly among native speakers living in many of the Anglosphere nations like the United States, Australia or the United Kingdom due to the worldwide perception that English speakers see little relevance in learning a second language. This is considered to be above all a result of the widespread distribution of English and its use as a lingua franca even in non-English speaking countries. According to Edwards (1994) the possession of a powerful language as English but also French, German or Spanish can lead to monolingual perspectives. The assumption that it is not necessary to learn a second language is based on the consideration that speakers of a minority group in a community need to learn the dominant language in order to accommodate to the majority and manage their everyday lives. Such notions have triggered off local discussions which deal with the question to which extent a non-native group should integrate its language and its culture into the public life of a community.

A good example illustrating this problem is the discussion in Germany about the integration of Turkish language and culture in everyday life. Due to the bad results in the PISA study which most of all uncovered the strong correlation between education and social background in Germany it has been proposed that German should be the obligatory language not only in lessons but also on the school grounds (Reimann 2006). This proposal on monolingualism at school is heavily disputed. With regard to cultural integration, there is for instance deep disagreement whether female teachers of Turkish nationality should be allowed to wear the traditional headscarf during their lessons. Monolingual perspectives also include the perception that bilingualism is something exotic with an either romantic or threadbare background since the speaker was either the child of European nobility or a child of refugees (Myers – Scotton 2003).

Myers-Scotton further claims that especially some Americans associate bilingualism with migrant and uneducated, unskilled workers.

In the end, monolingualism does not only describe the condition in which individuals only speak one language but furthermore a viewpoint which comes along with cultural narrowness which is often enforced by state policies attributing only one language an official status.

2.2 Bilingualism

It has already been mentioned that bilingualism is the standard rather than the exception these days. Individual as well as societal bilingualism has been promoted by several factors. Bilingualism derives from the contact between people with different nationalities whereas this contact can be forced under certain circumstances or chosen by the people themselves.

On the one hand, the geographical proximity between two communities is the reason for the development of bilingual communities and speakers. Close proximity between groups includes amongst others living in a border area between two nations. In border areas speakers often learn the language which is spoken across the frontier as being the case at the Dutch-German border. Moreover, close proximity also means living in a bilingual or multilingual area especially as a minority group. These conditions naturally call for the need to communicate with each other particularly for the purposes of trade. The marriage outside one's ethnic group is also a result from geographical proximity which then leads to the creation of bilingual families.

While close proximity on the one hand is a main factor for language contact, conditions of displacement (Myers-Scotton 2003) are another one. Due to certain events and developments throughout history, there are various reasons to explain migration of groups or an individual. An example for migration under force is the involuntary movement of Africans during the slave trade area to the Caribbean and southern states of America. This has resulted in the development of African American Vernacular English, a pidgin and creole language as a particular form of bilingualism. In addition, the movement of people to other countries has been a consequence of a prevalent war with the aim to seek political or religious refuge.

Another major historical factor explaining the development of bilingualism is colonialism since wielding power on the colonized nation also meant to impose the language of the conquerors on the local population. However, today the displacement of people does not exclusively occur under forced circumstances. The reasons to migrate in search of employment might be more or less voluntary. In some cases the economic situation of the home town certainly coerces people into moving away but there are also a number of people who leave their home town voluntarily. Due to economic as well as mental changes globalization has brought about, people are willing to learn additional languages in order to improve their occupational skills and therefore assure their mobility. This in particular applies to the learning of English for the purposes of international businesses. And apart from political or economic reasons there are still some people who learn additional languages out of curiosity and for the purposes of travelling.

Nevertheless, all these factors have finally resulted in the contact of people from different nationalities and therefore in the contact of different languages which has inevitably led to bilingualism.

In the history of bilingualism research various definitions have been proposed. Those have in common to use bilingualism as a cover term for speaking at least two or more languages. Yet, there is a distinction between societal and individual bilingualism. While the latter refers to the psychological state of an individual having access to two linguistic codes (Hamers; Blanc 2000), societal bilingualism is given when two languages are spoken in a community. This for instance used to be the case in Canada or Belgium.

Definitions on individual bilingualism have mainly differed in terms of proficiency meaning how fluent an individual can communicate in a second language. Narrow definitions such as the one of Leonard Bloomfield consider the perfect mastery of at least two languages as a criterion to define bilingualism. Thus, Bloomfield defines bilingualism as the "native-like control of two or more languages" (Apple/Muysken 1987:2). In contrast to that Mcnamara suggests that any person who possesses a minimal competence in only one of the four basic language skills (reading, writing, speaking, and listening) in another language than his mother tongue, can already be called a bilingual (Hamers; Blanc 2000). Whereas the above-mentioned descriptions are very limited and diverge extremely, the concept of bilingualism has become broader throughout the twentieth century and involves different degrees of competence in the languages that are involved.

According to Myers-Scotton (2003) for instance bilingualism does not imply the complete mastery of two languages and just a few bilinguals are as proficient in a second language as they are in their second. Bilingual speakers rarely achieve equal proficiency in both languages since they are, for the most part, not exposed to these languages to the same extent. In addition, the different languages are usually not used in the same situations and with the same frequency.

The difficulty in defining the term is to set a specific limit on the proficiency a speaker has to possess on a second language. Therefore, recent definitions as the one of Carol Myers-Scotton (2003) tend to define bilingualism in a very broad sense describing it as the "ability to use two or more languages sufficiently to carry on a limited casual conversation".

2.3 Multilingualism

Today it is very common to use the term multilingualism either instead of bilingualism or at least in the same context although the two terms do not exactly identify the same phenomenon. Bilingualism and multilingualism merely differ in the number of linguistic codes an individual or a community has access to. Thus, multilingualism describes the ability to speak more than two languages and comes about when speakers of different languages are brought together within the same political entity (Hoffmann 1991). Although there is barely a difference towards the concept of bilingualism, multilingualism remains a topic worth mentioning since in many parts of the world this phenomenon has become an indisputable fact of life.

Multilingualism on a societal level is particularly very common in Asian and African communities. Several languages co-exist in these countries and large sections of the population speak three or more languages. On the one hand, speakers use a local, ethnic or another indigenous language in order to communicate within their own or between different ethnic groups. Next to these local language speakers often use an additional language for more formal occasions. This language which may be, for instance, English, French or Spanish which has been introduced during the process of colonisation often serves as the language of education, bureaucracy and privilege (Wei 2000).

Attitudes towards multilingualism have also changed throughout history. With regard to societal multilingualism, many governments have chosen to ignore the linguistic diversity of their community in the past and gave only one language an official status (Hoffmann 1991). Nowadays the linguistic diversity of many countries is more or less accepted and there are some bilingual states, in which even two languages hold an official status. Brussels and Canada are the best known examples for states with two official languages. Nevertheless, the majority of multilingual communities still hold one official language and choosing this language can turn out to be a challenge for the government which then has to face possible internal conflicts especially if the nation has a colonial past.

Individual multilingualism is often regarded as an additional skill improving the occupational opportunities and mobility of the speaker. In many European countries, it is therefore very common today to learn at least two additional languages next to their mother tongue. The availability of different languages in a community can serve as a useful interactional resource for the multilingual speaker who usually assigns different roles to different languages. Thus, speakers may use one language in formal contexts as work, education and government and another one in more informal contexts with family and friends. The use of different languages is likely to occur in the same utterance. This very typical language behaviour performed by bilinguals or multilinguals is then known as code switching which will be the central subject matter in the following chapters.

3. Code switching

3.1 Language contact phenomena

In the previous chapter several occasions have been mentioned in which speakers of different languages communicate with each other. For the purposes of trade, amongst others, the linguistic exchange of speakers occurs very frequently with the consequence that their different languages influence each other. In other words, when speakers of different languages interact very closely with each other, this may result in a phenomenon which is called language contact. The permanent use of several languages in daily interaction can have different long-term effects on the grammars of those languages and the outcomes are defined as language contact phenomena which take many forms. Language contact phenomenon is used as a cover term for bilingual speech behaviour including code switching, borrowing, pidgin and creole development and the attrition of languages. All of these phenomena have in common that they are concerned with how elements of two different languages are used together and furthermore, they are concerned with the effects a grammar of one variety can have on the grammar of another variety (Myers-Scotton 2003).

Since the effects can be more or less radical language contact phenomena can be distinguished according to the degree of structural change obvious in the grammar. In other words, language contact phenomena range from the borrowing of words to more radical changes such as the attrition or total loss of a language or even to the development of pidgin and creole languages in communities in which speakers do not share any common language (Myers-Scotton 2002).

Among the various language contact phenomena it is above all the phenomenon of code switching that has attracted the attention of many linguists and has been studied from different perspectives.

3.2 General distinction between code switching and borrowing

In the previous chapter it has been explained that phenomena like code switching is one of many various language contact phenomena next to borrowing or pidginization. The diverse phenomena have may have the same origins, namely the contact between speakers of different language but still differ on a linguistic level. For further analysis it is necessary to keep code switching clearly from other language contact phenomena apart. A great deal of attention has been drawn to the distinction between code switching and borrowing. Gardner-Chloros claims that this can be explained with the frequent occurrence of single-word switching alongside with borrowing in many communities (1995).

Borrowing describes the process in which languages borrow words or phrases from other languages (Malmkjær 2002). One of the best known examples is the word *Computer* in German. The use of Anglicism especially in the media has led to the fact that those words which are in general called loanwords have established in the vocabulary of particular young speakers (Myers-Scotton 2003). Being widely accepted through their frequent use, loan words have become integrated into the recipient language of a community and are also perceived as a part of this. This is one important distinction between borrowing and code switching. Whereas loan words are integrated into the linguistic system of the other language and have established within the vocabulary of a linguistic community, words from the other language in code switching are used in their original sense. In contrast to borrowing, code switching is rather regarded as an individual and maybe spontaneous occurrence. In other words, the degree of integration is mainly used as a criterion to draw a line between the two language contact phenomena. Thus, it is assumed that loan words are adapted on a morphological as well as phonological level into the recipient language whereas words used in code switching are not (Apple/Muysken 1987). However, there is disagreement about the necessity of a sharp distinction of the terms due to the perception of some scholars that code switching can serve as a precursor borrowings (Carol Pfaff 1995). This means that foreign vocabulary introduced by code switching bear the potential of becoming a loan word. Nevertheless, the realm in which this debate is carried out implies a rather structural and grammatical perspective.

With regard to definitional issues it is sufficient and important to emphasize that code switching in contrast to other language contact phenomena such as borrowing describes an individual behaviour in which two different languages are used within the same conversation.

3.3 Definition of Code switching

The conversation between bilinguals is not always restricted to the use of one language. Bilingual speakers rather use their linguistic repertoire in an optimal way by switching between the languages which are available to them. This phenomenon is in linguistics well-known as code switching or code alternation. Code switching describes a very common and therefore central practise among bilingual speakers which can take many forms. Thus, the alternate use of two codes can occur within linguistic units of different length. Accordingly, it may occur within whole sentences, a part of a sentence or within single words or phrases. This means in particular that long blocks of speeches may be divided into parts which are expressed in different languages, a sentence may start in one language and finish in another one or words and phrases of one language are inserted in a sentence that is expressed in a different language (Wei 2000).

One of the first attempts to define code switching is made by Einar Haugen and Uriel Weinreich who are considered to have initiated code switching research. Here, the view of the bilingual speaker as someone who is equally proficient in both languages is relevant in order to understand their perception of code switching.

According to Weinreich

"The ideal bilingual switches from one language to the other according to appropriate changes in the speech situation (interlocutors, topics, etc.), but not in an un-
changed speech situation, and certainly not within a single sentence"

(1953:73,cited in Edel 2007)

Due to the perception that ideal bilinguals only switch between sentences a switching
within a sentence is therefore regarded as an interference phenomenon as part of a speech
behaviour performed by imperfect bilinguals. Code switching thus reflects the inability of the
speaker to carry on a conversation in one of the available languages.

Weinreich's understanding of code switching as interference which he describes as
"those instances of deviation from the norms of either language which occur in the speech of
bilinguals as a result of their familiarity with more than one language..." (Weinreich 1974:1,
cited in Edel 2007) supports this viewpoint. With regard to terms like interference it becomes
obvious that code switching has long been regarded as a lack of competence in one of the
languages which are available to bilingual speakers.

Although Haugen's and Weinreich's terminology and definitions have become widely
accepted and their view on code switching only reflected the attitudes of their time (Myers-
Scotton 1998), the understanding of bilingualism and therefore of code switching changed
fundamentally.

The widespread perception that codeswitching reveals the inability of bilinguals to express themselves adequately in one of the languages available to them proves to be wrong.
Since the seventies code switching is assumed to be a speech behaviour which requires a high
linguistic competence in a language (Edel 2007). Intensive studies on grammatical constraints
controlling code switching have shown that it is not just a simple combination of two different
grammars but the grammatical integration of one language into another one. The performance
of code switching therefore implies skilled manipulation of at least two overlapping sections
of grammar. The languages are not involved to the same extent since one language sets the
grammatical framework. This language is called the base, recipient or matrix language
(Malmkjær 2002). In contrast to that, the other language provides specific items which fits
into the framework of the base language. This language is characterized as the donor or
embedded language. Code switching passages have proved to be even in two typologically
different languages grammatically correct (Edel 2007). Due to this fact it does not simply

display the confusion of two languages but rather a complex form of bilingual communication.

Due to the changed perception of code switching more current definitions are rather general and basically agree with the fact that code switching is "the alternative use by bilinguals of two or more languages in the same conversation"(Milroy/Muysken 1995: 7). Milroy and Muysken use code switching as a cover term for different forms of bilingual behaviour. In other words, code switching can be distinguished according to its place of occurrence in a conversation. There are three different forms of code switching described in literature. On the one hand, this can involve the insertion of a tag in one language in a sentence which is expressed in another language. On the other hand, on a syntactical level there is a distinction between language alternation between sentences and alternation of languages within the sentence.

3.4 Types of code switching

Concerning the linguistic structures that are involved in code switching, Shana Poplack proposed a distinction between three different types of switching whereas all types can occur within the same discourse.

Tag switching or extra sentential codeswitching involves the insertion of a tag or an exclamation like 'you know' or 'I mean' in one language into a sentence which is otherwise in the other language (Romaine 1995). According to Suzanne such a tag may be easily inserted in an utterance and does not violate its syntactic structure.

Intersentential code switching describes a switch of language varieties at the sentence boundary or between the sentences. As a result one sentence or a part of a sentence can occur in one language and the following part in a different one as shown in the following example given by Poplack (1980, cited in Romaine 1995):

"Sometimes I'll start a sentence in Spanish *y termino en espangnol"*

According to Romaine intersentential code switching can be thought to require compared to tag switching a greater fluency in both languages since major parts of the utterance must conform to the syntactic rules of both languages.

In contrast to intersentential code switching the term intrasentential is used to refer to a switch within a sentence. More precisely, in intrasentential code switching the switch to a different language can either occur within clause boundary or even within the word boundary.

Intrasentential code switching is assumed to require the greatest fluency/proficiency in both languages. According to Romaine it bears the greatest risk of violating syntactic rules and is therefore often avoided even by fluent bilinguals.

All in all, code switching is defined as the alternation between at least two languages within a conversation, mostly by the same speaker. Whereas most of the definitions on code switching are referred to the alternation between languages in bilingual speech, it may also describe the alternation between dialects and styles in monolingual speech (Suzanne 1995). Due to the changing perception of code switching the definitions on code switching have become broader and less subjective. Accordingly, Myers-Scotton, for instance, defines the phenomenon of code switching in a more general way by describing it as the "alternations of linguistic *varieties* within the same conversation" (2003:241). However, for the purposes of this essay the definitions on code switching as the alternation of languages in bilingual speech is relevant.

4. The Sociolinguistic dimension of code switching

The study of codeswitching from a sociolinguistic point of view explores in particular the question why bilinguals perform codeswitching and in which situations a switch may be predictable. Although sociolinguists investigate the same questions they use different approaches in search of possible answers. In sociolinguistics, there is a basic distinction between macro-level approaches and micro-level approaches.

Macro level approaches, on the one hand, pay special attention to institutional and sociological categories which are prevalent in a linguistic community. These categories or boundaries are considered to be restricting to individual language behaviour. Accordingly, macro-level approaches explain individual language choices like code switching as derived from societal norms and structures. The individual behaviour of the interlocutors is exclusively regarded in terms of institutional, sociological categories and as a consequence of these factors.

Micro-level approaches, on the other hand, place their focus on the interlocutors of a conversation themselves and the relationship between them in order to draw conclusions on the meaning of speech behaviour.

Those linguists who apply micro-level approaches in order to explain the motivations behind codeswitching regard institutional and societal factors as insufficient or irrelevant to their goal. According to micro-level approaches it is the act of speaking itself and the speakers' values and communicative needs which are expressed through it that indeed gives meaning to language choices.

The chapter continues with introducing a study applying a macro-level perspective. Joshua Fishman's domain analysis serves as an appropriate example to explain the relation between society with its norms and expectations and individual language behaviour. He establishes a theory in which he tries to explain under which conditions or for which activities bilingual speakers are likely to choose a particular language.

4.1 Joshua Fishman's domain analysis

4.1.1. Language choice in a multilingual community

Joshua Fishman's analysis of multilingual settings is based on the question "Who speaks what language to whom and when?"(Wei 2000:60). The aim of the study is to discover and describe several analytic variables which contribute to an understanding of this question. Such a focus provides, on the one hand, stable bilingualism meaning that there is no shift from one language to another with the possible consequence of language loss and on the other hand, the existence of stable norms in a society which influence language choice and the habitual use of language (Hakuta 1999). The Puerto Rican community in Jersey served as an appropriate example for this purpose since their members were able to communicate proficiently in Spanish as well as in English. Fishman and his colleagues explored the general perception that bilingual speakers in a community use one language in a certain situation and the other language in another one. In order to do this, they observed the different conditions under which English and Spanish were used in Jersey. Resulting from the observations and interviews Fishman and his colleagues have made they came amongst others to the conclusion that the bilingual speakers of this community were very aware of their alternating language use. Consequently, speech behaviour such as codeswitching was not a random matter in a multilingual society. According to Fishman

> "Proper usage, or common usage, or both, dictate that only *one* of the theoretically co-available languages *will* be chosen by particular classes of *interlocutors* on particular *occasions*." (Fishman 1965:89)

Here, Fishman emphasizes that rather one language is the more appropriate one in a specific situation. He further refers to three main factors which influence the choice of language spoken in a conversation. Thus, the interlocutors of a conversation, the occasion including the place where it takes place and the topic the speakers are talking about determine the language choice. However, these factors cannot be regarded isolated from each other.

4.1.2 Factors determining language choice

Language choice is first of all determined by the speakers themselves and what attitudes and preferences those bring with them. The interlocutors of a conversation can be characterized by physiological features as age or gender as well as by sociological criteria as race, religion and status (Wei 2000). In addition, interlocutors characterize above all through their reference group membership. Fishman gives the example of a government functionary in Brussels who uses French at work, standard Dutch when having a drink at his club and a local variant of Flemish at home. This example reveals that the language choice of the government function-ary varies from one situation to the next. In each case the functionary identifies with the group to which he belongs to or from which he wants to gain approval by claiming his membership through the choice of the appropriate language. However, Fishman revises an exact one two one relationship between the reference group membership and the choice of language mean-ing that it is also possible that the government functionary could be addressed in French at his club. Thus, the existence of reference group is not necessarily a result of group-consciousness or awareness but must rather be regarded in dependence with the location and other environ-mental factors (Fishman 1965). Due to this fact, the concept of reference group membership leaves many exceptional cases. However, what is important about reference groups is that they reveal different relationships between interlocutors which in turn have an impact on the language choice in a conversation. In other words, a language will be chosen according to the degree of intimacy or formality which prevails in the relationship between the speakers and this particular degree of intimacy of formality between speakers is determined by the several reference groups (Hakuta 1999).

Another regulating factor influencing language choice is the concept of situation. Fish-man uses situation as a cover term which has been used to refer to a large variety of aspects. With regard to the participants these are according to Fishman aspects such as physical setting, topic and functions of a conversation as well as the style which is employed (Fishman 1965). Fishman concentrates for his purposes especially on the aspect of style, which can give a clue about the degree of intimacy or formality of a conversation. Moreover, style can reveal something about the status of an interlocutor or serve as a demonstration either power or solidarity. In other words, particular styles in different languages are considered to reveal the relationship between two interlocutors in terms of intimacy, formality and equality (Fishman 1965). So do bilinguals relate one of their languages more with informality, intimacy and equality than the other and consequently one particular language is more likely to be used in a certain situation than the other. Thus, in the Puerto Rican community in New Jersey a bilingual speaker may choose to speak English for rather formal occasions at work but Spanish in informal, more intimate interaction with family and friends.

Furthermore, topic is an important factor regulating language choice. There are several reasons why a change in topic can cause a switch to another language. Usually a speaker prefers to use a particular language for a certain topic based on the assumption that certain topics are better to handle in a specific language more than in the other one. This owes to the fact that bilingual speakers are seldom equally proficient in both languages. Therefore, a speaker may feel more competent to deal with a topic in one certain language since he or she has learnt the terminology according to this topic and is lacking the appropriate terms for a satisfying conversation in the other language. Another reason might be that the speaker might think that a language does not possess the appropriate terms for a certain topic and the other language is then simply considered to be the better language for speaking about this particular topic. (Hakuta 1999).

Although interlocutor, situation and topic remain relevant factors that influence language choice they are according to Haberland (2005) not sufficient in themselves to explain choice patterns. Therefore, Fishman introduced the term domain as an analytical concept.

4.1.3 What is a domain?

In the course of their observations Fishman and his colleagues made in the Puerto Rican speech community they identified five domains, in which either English or Spanish were permanently spoken. These domains governing language choice were the family, friendship, religion, employment and education and served as "anchor points for distinct value systems which are embodied in the use of Spanish as opposed to English" (Romaine 2000:44).

The domain analysis refers to a concept that was usually suggested by Schmidt - Rohr in the 1930ies with the purpose to identify the different areas of language use which are relevant for language choice in a multilingual society (Haberland 2005). Fishman took up the idea of domains in the seventies when he analysed multilingual settings. He defines domain as a "cluster of social situations typically constrained by a common set of behavioural rules" (Fishman 1965: 89). A domain therefore does not only describe a specific setting or a situation but is above all determined by the conditions of its social environment. The school or university, for instance, is first of all a location but becomes a domain or a "social situation" in concurrence with the prevalent role relations between the involved persons like lecturers, teachers and students as well as with corresponding topics like exams. Accordingly, a domain establishes above all through what Fishman describes as "a common set of behavioural rules". His quote clarifies the impact and meaning of societal norms that rule the participants' patterns of behaviour which in turn determine the social situation. In other words, a domain is not given beforehand but depends on its context in which it occurs. According to Fishman, each domain in a bilingual community carries different expectations for using Spanish and English and is associated with a particular variety of language (Hakuta 1999). In the Puerto Rican community so to speak, English and Spanish are used in different contexts and therefore serve different functions for the individual speaker in his or her speech community. Put differently, a particular language identifies a domain. In order to support this claim Fishman and his colleagues conducted further studies in which they constructed hypothetical conversations which differed in terms of interlocutors, topic and situation. The following chart illustrates that each domain reveals a specific role relationship existing between the interlocutors. According to these role relationships, Fishman suggests probable settings where this conversation takes place and congruent topics speakers may discuss.

Domain	Interlocutor	Place	Topic
Family	Parent	Home	How to be a good son or daughter
Friendship	Friend	Beach	How to play a certain game
Religion	Priest	Church	How to be a good Christian
Education	Teacher	School	How to solve an Algebra problem
Employment	Employer	Workplace	How to do your job more effectively

The Scheme of Relationships in Fishman's (1972) Domain Analysis

(Boztepe 2005:13)

Finally, a domain is a theoretical concept which is able to explain the correlation between a language choice and certain types of activities. These activities represent a combination of certain role relationships, settings and topics. According to Haberland (2005) the power of domains lie in their predictive force meaning that they possess the ability to suggest which language a speaker might choose in a given situation. With regard to the Puerto Rican community in New Jersey, Spanish speakers are thus predicted to use English in formal and work-related domains based on the associations of English with institutional activities whereas Spanish is expected to be used with informal activities (Milroy/Gordon 2003). Yet, the number of domains can vary from community to community and domains themselves are subject to change since bilingual situations are not entirely stable (Myers-Scotton 2003). According to this, Fishman stresses that domains always have to be concluded from careful observation of the linguistic group.

4.2 Code switching at an interactional level

Although Fishman's work continued to be influential, many researchers continued to study language behaviour by employing a micro-level perspective. According to that, not overall societal norms but the speakers themselves give social meaning to code switching. Similar to Fishman John J. Gumperz assumes that topic, interlocutors and situation are important factors that have an impact on language use but in contrast to Fishman he concentrated in particular on the interactive strategies bilingual speakers use within a conversation. In the course oh his study, Gumperz arrived at a list of several functions code switching has for the discourse itself and introduces. The studies conducted by Jan Blom and John J. Gumperz in Hemnesberget, Norwegian are considered to have stimulated the interest in code switching as a respectable research topic. With concentrating on code switching between dialects of Norwegian in Hemnesberget in, a Norwegian fishing village, Blom and Gumperz stimulated a "flood of investigation of CS between languages" (Myers - Scotton 1998: 46). Thus, Gumperz is regarded as one of the most influential linguists in the discussion for the social motivations of code switching during the 1970ies and later on.

4.2.1 The discourse functions of code switching (Blom & Gumperz)

4.2.1.1 The 'we-code' and 'they-code'

An important distinction on which Gumperz's approach relies on is the distinction between the languages which bilingual speakers use since the different perception of certain languages in society may give a clue about the motivations which are beyond a particular language choice. Gumperz assumes that the languages which are available to bilinguals resemble the contrasting cultural standards of the minority community and larger society with which these are associated (1982). He introduces the terms 'we code' and 'they code' in order to describe the different status or prestige those languages have in society. Put differently, the statuses of different languages reflect the structural differences in the society itself. In general, Gumperz makes a distinction between languages with a high status and languages with a low status.

On the one hand, he uses the term 'we code' in order to describe the minority language or often the ethnic language which is used with more informal activities as they might occur between family and friends. On the other hand, the term 'they code' is used to refer to the majority language in a community. This language is associated with more formal and less personal out-group activities as it occurs for example at work (Gumperz 1982). Thus, 'we' and 'they' codes resemble the group identity of a bilingual speaker or to use Fishman's terminology, the reference group membership. Whereas Fishman has claimed that there is no exact one-to-one relationship between the reference group and language, Gumperz either adds that the distinction he has made is a rather symbolic one has no predictive value.

4.2.1.2 Situational and metaphorical code switching

Based on their studies conducted in Hemnesberget, a small settlement Norway with the aim to explore code switching between related varieties, Blom and Gumperz observed that the selection of distinct codes was constrained by social events which are defined in terms of participants, setting. More particularly, code switching was triggered in general by a "shift in topic and in other extralinguistic context markers that characterize the situation" (Gumperz 1982: 98). That means that in a specific situation a certain code seems to be more appropriate than the other one may be. Thus, speakers need to change their choice of language to keep up with the changes in situational factors and in doing so, speakers are able to maintain this appropriateness (Wei 1995). They drew this conclusion amongst others from teachers who reported that they would treat a lecture in contrast to a discussion as a different situation. Whereas lectures were hold in the standard dialect *Bokmål*, the regional dialect *Ranamål* was chosen when teachers intended to encourage open discussion.

In order to describe this kind of shift in which the alternation of linguistic codes implies a changed social situation, Blom and Gumperz introduced the term situational switching. Situational code switching still reveals the proximity to Fishman's domain concept since both assume that only one language or style is related to a certain kind of activity or is considered to be more appropriate in a particular situation than the other one. Besides, with situational code switching Blom and Gumperz refer to a switch between languages or varieties that is motivated by the changing factors external to the participants' own motivations (Myers-Scotton 1993). Situational switching can already be triggered when only one of the factors that constitutes a situation such as topic, interlocutor or setting changes. According to the new situation different role relations, rights and obligations of the interlocutors are redefined for each other (Boztepe 2005). According to this, a change of the participant constellation could, for instance, lead from the use of a 'we code' to speaking a 'they code'.

Metaphorical switching is in contrast to the latter not exclusively triggered by a change in situation but involves the use of two languages within one social setting with the same interlocutors. The term describes a switch of a speaker with the intention to achieve a special communicative effect and to convey meaning through the choice of language. Thus, the speaker may switch to another language in order to change the tone of a conversation, to emphasize a certain part the conversation or to make a comment on a situation in a different language. This may happen with the intention to call for a certain attitude of the addressee or according to Myers – Scotton for "the presentation of self *in relation to* topic, or changes in relationship to other participants" (1993: 52). From recorded conversations between adults and a group of university students Blom and Gumperz observed that metaphorical switching is not only motivated by the topic but the use of the standard dialect further implies the interlocutors' shared experiences as students so that the change from one language to another may serve as an expression of trust and solidarity (Myers-Scotton 1993).

4.2.1.3 Conversational code switching

The terms situational and metaphorical code switching were introduced in a collection of readings on sociolinguistics called *Directions in Sociolinguistics* edited by Gumperz and Dell Hymes in 1972. In a further collection of essays on code switching called *Discourse Strategies* which Gumperz edited ten years later, he extended his earlier ideas and introduced the term conversational code switching. The term conversational code switching already indicates that Gumperz focuses in particular on the discourse function of language alternation which he defines "as the juxtaposition within the same speech exchange of passages of speech belonging to two different grammatical systems or subsystems." (1982: 59)

First of all, Gumperz compares conversational code switching to the language situation that is given in diglossia. The term was first used by Ferguson in order to describe two different varieties of the same languages existing in a speech community. The main idea underlying this concept is that speakers use only one variety in a particular situation. A switch between single varieties can thus be compared to what Gumperz describes as situational switching. However, Gumperz claims that in comparison to this situational type of switching conversational code switching is more complex since the speakers are less aware of which code they use on a particular occasion and are rather concerned with the communicative effect that they want to achieve (1982). According to this, conversational code switching displays certain features that has been covered under the term metaphorical switching so far. However, Gumperz emphasizes that it is far more reasonable that speakers build on their own understanding of situational norms than using language according to fixed norms given in a society and thus distances himself from macro-level categories. In order to identify and isolate the functions of conversational code switching, a close analysis of the discourse itself is necessary. Based on various language contact situations throughout the world such as in North India, Austria or the United States he arrives at a list of six basic discourse functions conversational code switching may have.

First of all, a switch to another language can mark a distinction between direct and indirect speech in an utterance. More precisely, code switching passages can be identified either as a direct *quotation* in a different language or as reported speech (Gumperz 1982). Thus, a sentence expressed in Spanish by one speaker may be directly quoted or reported in English by another speaker.

Addressee specification is another function achieved through code switching. Here the choice of another language aims at directing a message to a particular person, a particular addressee among other persons who are present in the immediate environment and therefore possible addressees. Romaine further adds that this kind of switch can be regarded as an invitation to participate in the conversation (1995).

Code switching and in this particular case tag switching can further serve to mark an *interjection* or sentence filler. Accordingly, expressions in a particular language are inserted into a sentence which is expressed in a different language.

Moreover, speakers may switch to language in order to repeat what has just been said in a different language. By repeating the utterance speakers can either clarify or emphasize a message (Gumperz 1982). In this context, code switching functions as *reiteration*.

Code switching as *message qualification* occurs when a main message is expressed in one language and followed by an elaboration or qualification in the other language. Yet, Romaine (1995) suggests the terms topic and comment in order to describe message qualification within a conversation. Thus, a topic may be introduced in English and commented further on in Spanish.

Finally, code switching as *personalization versus objectivization* indicates the degree to which a speaker is involved or distant from a message or whether a statement reflects the personal opinion or a fact. A statement expressed in Spanish can be, for instance, more personal and used for *acting out* specific problems whereas the use of English reflects more distance and is rather used to *talk about* these problems (Gumperz 1982).

Whereas some of these functions like quotation marking or interjections are more concerned with the structural elements of a statement, other functions display the speaker's personal motivation as in the case of addressee specification. Identifying and isolating the discourse functions of conversational code switching is according to Gumperz (1982) the first important step in code switching analysis since it provides categories which can be employed in discussing the problems of interpretation. But he also adds that the identification of discourse functions alone is not sufficient to explain the motivations of the speakers involved in a conversation and external factors can always be taken into consideration. Finally, he claims that similar interpretations on the meaning of code switching allow for the conclusion that code switching works as a part of contextualization cues which will be the subject to deal with in the next subchapter.

4.2.1.4. Code switching as a contextualization cue

With regard to the interpretation of conversational code switching Gumperz refers to the notion of contextualization cues. He argues that

> [...] conversational interpretation is cued by empirically debatable signs, contextualiza-
> tion cues, and that the recognition of what these signs are, how they relate to grammati-
> cal signs, how they draw on socio-cultural knowledge and how they affect understand-
> ing, is essential for creating and sustaining conversational involvement and therefore to
> communication as such. (Gumperz 1992: 42)

These cues or signs can range from the participant's activities and devices such as into-
nation, speech rhythm and code switching to non-verbal aspects of communication like
gestures and gaze which all have the function to mark the conversation. Contextualization
cues are on the one hand used in the production of language and at the same time used for
the interpretation of this since they provide the context the listener needs in order to understand the speaker's meaning. In other words, listeners can find social meaning in a conversation by paying attention to various hints or cues which are embedded in the discourse
(Myers-Scotton 2003).

Conversational code switching, in particular, serves amongst other linguistic activities
as a contextualization cue since it can mark a conversation by creating a contrast between
two passages of speech. In engaging in code switching, bilinguals exploit their ability to
choose between different codes of their linguistic repertoire in order "signal contrast between
what has been said (by themselves or others) and what they are about to say"(Dimitrijević
2004: 38). Due to the concept of contextualization the choice of a new language and the
resulting contrast conveys a specific meaning that has to be interpreted by the listener.
However, the correct interpretation of code switching requires a shared or similar linguistic
perception of the interlocutors since the choice of another language would otherwise lead to
misunderstandings. Nevertheless, it is important to emphasize that these cues do not work
isolated from each other but may occur mutually. Code switching serves as one of many
means among others to contextualize functions such as emotion, perspective or judgement.
According to this, bilingual speaker possess even more means of contextualization than
monolingual speakers do. Those, in comparison, can mark their speech with the help of
stylistic means whereas bilingual speakers have access to all the above mentioned devices.
Furthermore, by regarding code switching as a contextualization cue Gumperz emphasizes

that code switching is not a random behaviour but a rather functional, meaningful use of the linguistic resources which the participants use to realize their communicative needs.

4.2.2 Code switching within conversational analysis (Peter Auer)

Peter Auer is the best known linguist to have further developed John J. Gumperz interactional perspective by introducing conversation analysis theory for the study of code switching. Auer refers to Gumperz concept of contextualization and emphasizes that the central idea of this theory is that language is not only determined by its context but in turn creates the context (1999). Central to Auer's understanding of context is that

> "[…] it is not something given a priori and influencing or determining linguistic details; rather it is shaped, maintained and changed by the participants continually in the course of interaction." (Auer 1992:80?)

Auer questions the way context or situation has been defined so far. For him, it is a predetermined set of norms constraining language behaviour but an interactively achieved phenomenon (Wei 1998). This is a very important statement on which his he backs his approach on puts.

Conversation analysis as a method which Auer uses in order to describe the functions of code switching is based on the approach of ethnomethodology. This approach studies the relation between the knowledge of social actors about interaction and their procedures and methods in daily interaction (Malmkjær 2002). This knowledge is constructed through conversation and thus through language. Sharing this assumption conversation analysis aims at discovering the structures of talk in which especially the organisation of speech sequences produce social meaning and action (Malmkjær 2000). According to this, Auer puts particular emphasis on the sequential environment of code switching meaning that a switch and the meaning it conveys must be analysed according to its preceding as well as to its following utterances. The importance of this condition for him becomes very obvious when he claims that

> Any theory of conversational code-alternation [his term] is bound to fail if
> it does not take into account that the meaning of code alternation depends
> in essential ways on its 'sequential environment (Auer 1995:116).

With sequential environment Auer refers to the preceding and following language choices which must be considered in the interpretation of code alternation. He claims that this meaning embedded in conversation is relative independent from its social meaning for the community (1995). Accordingly, Auer distances himself from the widespread perception of macro-sociolinguists that social meaning is predetermined by external, situational factors and there-fore downplays the role of societal norms with regard to language choice. Instead, he empha-sizes that social meaning is "locally produced "and therefore constructed within the conversa-tion itself. In other words, the context is regarded as the outcome of the interaction and this in turn is relevant for the interpretation of the meaning or message. Thus, special attention must be paid to the general organization of the discourse with particular emphasis on the sequences in which codes alternate. The appropriate analytic tool for this purpose is the method of conversation analysis since it is only possible to catch the details of linguistic processes by meticulous transcription. With regard to the interpretation of code alternation as a contextuali-sation cue, Auer distinguishes the following types of code alternation according to their specific functions in the discourse.

4.2.2.1 Discourse –related code switching

The first type is defined as discourse-related switching and is according to Martin-Jones speaker-oriented (1995). This kind of alternation has the function to contribute to the organi-sation of the discourse in a particular episode and is usually interpreted by the participant to contextualize a particular feature of the interaction. For instance, code switching may contex-tualize a shift in topic or a change in the participant constellation (Auer 1995). In order to clarify the function of discourse-related switching, Auer presents the following example in which an informal conversation between Spanish-German bilingual speakers takes place. In the conversation a female student asks her male fellow student for the time by using Spanish (Spanish in italics):

1		(25.0)
2	W	*qué hora es ?*
		('what time is it?')
3		(2.0)
4	→	wie spät?
5	M	zwanzig nach elf;
		('twenty past eleven;')
6	W	h (2.5)
7	M	wann muß du hoch?
		(,when do you have to go?'[i.e. to the university])

8   W   nö – nich so früh. Ich hab erst um vier uni

(Tilmann Altenberg, unplished data 1992 cited in Auer 1998: 4-5)

On the one hand, this example reveals how a conversation analysis transcript works. The numbers in brackets represent the stretches of silence in seconds. The arrow in line 4 marks the point of the conversation at which code switching takes place. On the other hand, the function of code switching for the effectiveness of the conversation becomes obvious. The fact that the fellow student is not responding to the question expressed in Spanish (which becomes obvious through the pause in line 3) is being interpreted as the wrong language choice by the female speaker. In order to receive the required answer and to keep the conversation going she engages in code switching by repeating the question in German. Here, code switching in this sequential position serves as a "second attempt" (Auer 1998:5) to initiate a question and to contribute to the organization of the discourse.

However, Auer adds that although he focuses in particular on the conversational structure the knowledge of external factors which are for instance factors about culture and society are necessary to reach a full understanding of code switching.

4.2.2.2 Participant and preference –related code switching

Some code alternations leave according to Auer language choice open meaning that it is not clear which language is the one to continue with in the conversation. Auer claims that keeping the language choice open provides information about the speaker as a person and about his or her conceptualisation of the situation (1995).Therefore, this kind of language alternation is considered to be participant-related. Whereas discourse-related code switching generates meaning with regard to the organisation of talk, participant-related code switching generates meaning about the involved participants (Gafaranga 2007). Thus, the latter leads to conclusions about the speaker or listener. According to this, Auer refers to language preference or preference-related code switching. Such a switch reveals as the term already indicates the speaker's preference of one language rather than the other in a particular context. Yet, the motivations and reasons for this preference-related may be different whereas Auer emphasizes that the preference is not psychologically motivated but rather technical (1998). On the one hand, a language is chosen due to the linguistic competence of the speaker. In this case, speakers may prefer to speak the language in which they feel more competent in and thus avoid to speak the language in which in which they feels insecure. On the other hand, a preferred switch can be the result of a conscious decision which is based on political considerations such as it was and is for the post part apparent in Canada (Auer 1995). In this case, language alternation reveals according to Gafaranga an ideological preference (2007).

4.3 Socio-psychological motivations for code switching

In the previous chapter the focus was set on approaches that either declare societal norms and categories as responsible for language choices or view the speakers' attitudes and the conversation itself as explaining factors for the construction of social meaning.

The following approaches reconsider in the psychological forces within the individuals which may cause language behaviour such as code switching. Socio-psychological approaches are unlike the approaches we have explored so far based on the assumption that language choices cannot be explained sufficiently by entirely referring to the situational factors and categories of a society. Explanations for language choice have to take aspects of interpersonal relationship and the psychological forces which influence an individual's behaviour into consideration (Appel/Muysken 1987). Thus, some researchers consider code switching within communication accommodation theory (CAT) formerly known as speech accommodation theory (SAT) set up by Howard Giles and his colleagues. The term has been modified since Giles and his associates intended to include all aspects of communicative behaviour like prosody etc. into their model (Myers-Scotton 2003). Since this is a discussion on code switching as a feature of bilingual speech will therefore refer to the term speech accommodation. Speech accommodation theory as one attempt to explain language choices in general claims that speakers make language choices in order to accommodate their speech to persons with the aim of convergence or divergence.

Carol Myers-Scotton either concentrates on the psychological motivations within the speakers but she claims to be rather concerned with the speaker's own goals and not with the addressee (2003). Moreover, the markedness model is regarded as an attempt to include both macro- and micro level perspective.

4.3.1 Speech accommodation theory (SAT)

4.3.1.1 What does accommodation mean?

The adaptation of two speakers two each other's speech is a relevant feature of interpersonal communication. Accommodation is a very common behaviour and can occur in everyday situations e.g. when we tend to speak more slowly during a conversation with a foreigner or when we use "baby talk" which is grammatically simple language with young children. In other words, accommodation which may occur in monolingual as well as in bilingual speech is concerned with how speakers use, evaluate and alter their speech styles in face-to-face interaction (Fishman 1999).

Based on dialect studies which led to the conclusion that people are judged by the way they speak Giles and his associates went on to study under what circumstances speakers change the way they speak and developed the Speech Accommodation theory explaining language choices. The assumption on which the model is based is that speakers are likely to make linguistic choices in order to become more alike to other speakers or otherwise define their difference to them. By speaking a particular language they adjust their speech style with others in order to express certain attitudes, values and intentions (Street/Giles 1982, cited in Redmond n.d.). Furthermore, Communication Accommodation Theory is concerned with the motivations for such behaviour and the resulting consequences. The model focuses on the cognitive processes underlying the speaker's perception of a conversation and his communicative behaviour. More precisely, speech accommodation theory is based on the following social psychological processes (Hamers/Blanc 2000):

(1) Similarity attraction
(2) Social exchange
(3) Causal attribution
(4) Intergroup distinctiveness

Similarity attraction is a mechanism which has the effect that an individual feels more attracted to another person when they have similar attitudes and beliefs. Accommodating to one's speech means to reduce linguistic differences between the speaker and his addressee and therefore increases the attraction since the addressee will perceive him as more similar to him. Furthermore, accommodation results from the mechanisms of social exchange through which the speaker tries to weigh the relative costs and rewards of an interaction. In other words, a speaker will accommodate his speech given that the rewards of his accommodation are higher than the costs. The costs of accommodation through a switch to another language can be, for instance, regarded as a threat to the ethnic identity (Hamers/Blanc 2000). In contrast to that, the rewards gained by this behaviour may show in the social approval of the addressee. With regard to the listener the psychological process of causal attribution serves as an explanation why convergent accommodation is perceived as a purpose to reduce the social distance between the interlocutors. Causal attribution describes the mechanism through which a listener interprets a speaker's behaviour according to his motives and intentions he attributes to this behaviour (2000). Moreover, the process of intergroup distinctiveness influences speech accommodation as well. The underlying assumption is that when members of two groups come in contact they tend to compare themselves on several relevant dimensions and these comparisons in turn serve the individual to forge their group image and positive in-group distinctiveness (Thanasoulas 1999). Speech accommodation can serve as a tool for distinguishing oneself from members of other groups with the aim to either call attention to the own group or to support it. Reconsidering the above-mentioned psychological motivations underlying this behaviour it becomes obvious that the concept of speech accommodation takes note of two contrary tendencies.

On the one hand, speakers tend to accommodate their speech to persons whom they like or whom they wished to be liked by. In this particular case, speech convergence is performed by the individual. On the other hand, speakers may tend to diverge and create the desired level of social distance from persons whom they don't like. This, on the other hand, is achieved through speech divergence.

4.3.1.2 Switching for convergence

Speakers are motivated to make changes in their speech in order to be evaluated more or less favourably by their listeners. One way of converging one's speech is to choose the language which suits the needs of the interlocutor for the purpose of an effortless conversation (Apple/Muysken 1987). As a result the speaker makes the other person more confident who is in turn more willing to respond. Thus, convergence first of all evokes positive reactions and can be regarded as a means to improve the effectiveness of a conversation. There are several factors that influence this for the most part unconscious behaviour. On an interpersonal level the movement towards another communication style is regarded to as a means to means to satisfy the speaker's desire for social approval and liking (Fishman 1999). He or she may even try to identify with the listener by switching from his mother tongue to the language both have in common.

However, accommodation does not only apply to individual speakers but can also be discussed on a societal level. In multilingual communities, there is normally a dominant group with more political and economic power which has the position to impose their language on the subordinate group. Members of the subordinate group and above all immigrants will usually learn and use the language of the dominant group for conversations in out-group situations. Thus, accommodation (Myers-Scotton 2003) to the dominant group's language is likely to result in a specific language choice or code switching. Myers-Scotton claims that the reasons for this accommodation are of a psychological as well as of an instrumental nature (2003). A psychological reason is that individuals want to belong to a group. Speakers see themselves as a member of the same group or would like to be considered as a member of this. An instrumental reason for convergence is to improve the social and economic chances of the individual. Consequently, speech convergence turns out to be not only a very common but also necessary behaviour to guarantee and improve one's social and economic mobility. Nevertheless, speech convergence is according to Myers- Scotton also the reason why the mother tongue of immigrants is often lost by the third generation (2003).

4.3.1.3 Switching for divergence

Divergent accommodation in form of code switching works in the opposite direction to convergent accommodation. Divergence may be result from the contempt a speaker has for another person or his behaviour and from the desire to remain different from this person. In other words, a speaker who consciously switches to another speech style may have the intention to create or maintain the social distance between him and the listener by accentuating their linguistic differences (Myers-Scotton 1993). On a conversational level, a shift to another language might be performed with the intention to simply avoid the engagement in a lengthy discussion with the interlocutor.

Nevertheless, divergence can be also practised in group relation and occurs towards rather undesirable groups (Redmond n.d.). On the one hand, an undesirable group may be the more powerful and dominant language group in a society which has achieved its status through the process of colonizing. In this particular case, the members of the colonized minority group want to distinguish themselves by using their native language and abandoning the language of the colonizer. On the other hand, an undesirable group may be that with a lower educational status. Members of an elite group want to distinguish from this group by using a language with a high prestige (Myers-Scotton). In both cases, speech divergence fulfils an identity function. Based on the psychological process of intergroup distinctiveness, speech divergence has the function to define and accentuate the linguistic differences between two groups. Thus, a speaker diverges in order to distinguish himself as a member from a particular group from the other participant by the choice of his or her language. Accordingly, language serves as the main tool to reinforce the individual identity as well as the group identity. Due to the motivations underlying speech divergence it is assumed that this kind of accommodation is in comparison to convergence behaviour speakers are very aware of. According to this it can be concluded that code switching when it aims at divergence is a rather conscious behaviour and not a random action.

4.3.2 The markedness model (MM)

Carol Myers-Scotton's Markedness model which she introduced in the 1980ies is not only an effort to identify the social and psychological motivations underlying code switching but furthermore serves as an attempt to include macro-level perspectives and micro-level perspectives into the research of code switching. That means in particular that she draws her conclusions from conversations she has amongst others observed between bilingual speakers of Swahili and English in Kenya. However, by analysing the data she also takes societal norms which have an influence on language choice into consideration. Myers – Scotton herself claims her model to incorporate several themes from a variety of disciplines such as from sociolinguistics, pragmatics, and social anthropology which have all in common that they emphasize the speaker as a creative actor and regard the linguistic choices as accomplishing rather than conveying of referential meaning (1998). The point of introducing this model is in establishing a method which speakers and listeners can make use of in order to judge linguistic choices they consider to be more or less marked in an interaction (Myers-Scotton 2003). She further claims that the Markedness model in contrast to other models like speech accommodation theory is more concerned with the speaker's own intentions whereas in speech accommodation theory language speakers make their choice dependent of the participants' approval or disapproval.

In her attempt to explore the psychological and social motivations that lead to code switching Myers Scotton asks the following question:

> What do speakers gain by conducting a conversation in two languages (i.e. through code switching) rather than simply using one language? (1993:3)

4.3.2.1 Rights and Obligations set (RO)

A very important assumption this approach is based is that there are fixed patterns of role relationships between the interlocutors deriving from societal norms that determine an appropriate social and linguistic behaviour within a society and the shared linguistic experience within a society leads to the conventionalising of such an interaction (Wei 1995)

As a consequence, a pattern of expected rights and obligations of the interlocutors establishes. This pattern which is based on the situational factors and the common experiences speakers have made in a society is referred to as Rights and Obligations as part of the normative expectations which exists for each type of interaction and exists for each speaker (Myers-Scotton 2003). This theoretical construct refers to what participants can expect in any given interaction type such as a conversation in a community. Thus, the term rights and obligations is not to be understood in a literally sense but is rather used in terms of norms of the speech behaviour and attitudes that have established in a speech community. Here, it is important to add that the RO sets are specific for each community meaning that they can differ from community to community (Myers-Scotton 1993).

4.3.2.2 Unmarked choices

In order to make judgements about linguistic choices of a participant at all, speakers must possess the necessary communicative competence, a concept that was introduced by Dell Hymnes in the 1970ies (Myers-Scotton 1993). According to this concept competent speakers of a language own in addition to their grammatical competence which refers to the understanding, knowledge and production of grammatical correct utterances, a communicative competence (Malmkjær 2002). This competence refers to the ability of speakers to use these grammatically correct utterances appropriately. Therefore the speaker must know beforehand, in which social situation an utterance is appropriate or not. According to Myers-Scotton this competence is on the one hand based on innate structures but also includes stored and assembled knowledge in the course of language (2003). With regard to this competence as well as to the experiences made by speakers in a community bilinguals develop a sense of what may be an appropriate or inappropriate language choice in a specific type of interaction. Myers-Scotton uses the term unmarked instead of appropriate when she describes linguistic choices that are more or less expected in a conversation. Thus "the unmarked choice is the linguistic reflection of any specific RO set, but only in a specific interaction type." (2003: 159)

That means that the unmarked or appropriate choice in code switching is the expected one by the addressee because that particular choice reveals the norms and behavioural rules which are prevalent in a speech community. In other words, a speaker does not violate or offend conversational rules and is on the safe side by choosing the unmarked choice. Myers – Scotton claims that community norms determine what an unmarked behaviour is and that these norms and values in turn are conveyed by the members of communities whereas family and friends convey in-group values and the colleagues at work or authorities may commit out-group values (1993). This explanation reveals the influence of Joshua Fishman's domain analysis because at this point Myers-Scotton emphasises the meaning of societal factors for the choice of language in code switching.

4.3.2.3 Marked choices and the negotiation principle

Since this model is called markedness model the marked choices in code switching are of greater interest. In contrast to unmarked choices marked choices are those who are not predicted in a conversation. In order to understand why speakers make a marked choice it is necessary to explain the underlying principle of this theory, the negotiation principle that states:

> Choose the form of your conversation contribution such that it indexes the set of rights and obligations which you wish to be in force between speaker and addressee for the current exchange (Myers-Scotton 1993: 113)

This principle claims that the speakers' motivations are responsible for code choices und that a marked choice reveals a negotiation for an RO set. This principle provides the basis for the markedness model of code switching as well as of the following related maxims under the model (1998):

(1) Unmarked Choice Maxim

(2) Marked Choice Maxim

(3) Exploratory Choice Maxim

Myers –Scotton claims that speakers have these maxims in mind when they make a language choice. As already mentioned in the previous chapter, speakers follow the (1) unmarked choice maxim when they intend to affirm the prevalent rights and obligations set. In contrast to that, speakers make a (2) marked choice when they intend to establish a new rights and obligations set. Thus, marked choices imply that the speakers do not identify with the expected rights and obligations set. They choose a marked choice or in other words, an unexpected language in order to call for a new situation, a new RO set in which the marked choice in turn becomes the unmarked choice (2003). Consequently, a speaker choosing an unexpected language also redefines the role relationships between the speakers. Next to the unmarked and marked choice there is (3) the exploratory choice maxim. The latter is applied when the unmarked choice is not clear and the speaker is uncertain about which language choice is the expected one or will help him to achieve his communicative intent.

In following these maxims the speakers often engage in code switching. As a result, the following types of code switching which are applied to achieve different goals are distinguished according to those maxims the speaker has in mind.

4.3.2.4 Code switching as an unmarked choice

Here Myers-Scotton differentiates between sequential unmarked code switching and code switching as the unmarked choice itself. The former is triggered by a change in situational factors e.g. a shift in the topic within the course of a conversation (1993). Due to this change the unmarked rights and obligations set may also change and therefore the speaker may switch codes in order to adjust to this new situation. This kind of switch is similar to what Gumperz has defined as situational switching. In doing so the speaker then accepts the present state.

Code switching itself can serve as an unmarked choice which means that the switching between two languages is very frequent and common in a particular community and may carry as an overall pattern its own meaning. Speakers switch between languages very constantly with the aim to emphasize their "dual identities" or memberships in both ethnic groups and cultures which are indicated by the languages (2003). This is according to Myers-Scotton very common in communities of Great Britain where highly educated immigrants from India make their code switching their unmarked choice for in-group conversations. Those speakers use English at work but switch between their native language e.g. Hindi and English at home and with members from their own ethnic group. Thus, bilingual speakers use code switching as a means to retain to their ethnic group on the hand and to adapt to their culture where they live now (2003).

4.3.2.5 Marked choices in code switching

In case of code switching as a marked choice the speaker does not accept the present state of a conversation and calls for a new rights and obligations set. The motivation behind this behaviour is to indicate a change in the relationship between the participants in the conversation. In engaging in code switching speakers can express feelings ranging from anger to affection or lead to outcomes ranging from the power dimension to that of solidarity showing in demonstrations of authority, superiority as well of ethnic identity (Myers-Scotton 1993).

Very often code switching is used to express one's authority in many different ways. This can amongst others go along with feelings like anger with the intention to intimidate the addressee. In addition, demonstrating one's authority by using a language which is not the unmarked choice can also have the intention to exclude the participant from the conversation. According to Myers-Scotton, marked code switching serves as an ethnically- based exclusion strategy (1993).

Rather with a sense to impress the addressee than intimidating him, speakers who employ code switching want to show how modern and multidimensional they are. This may for example occur between people engaged in commerce. Myers-Scotton gives an example in which a seller may speak the customer's language in order to keep up the sales conversation, to signify politeness and to associate with him (2003). However, by switching between two or more languages the seller wants to impress the customer and to claim his educated and therefore powerful status showing that he as a person or as well the company he is representing is modern, multidimensional and has an international status.

Moreover, code switching as a marked choice can serve as a demonstration of solidarity and group membership. Myers–Scotton draws this conclusion from observations between a Kenyan trilingual accountant and his client. Both have the same ethnic background and English as lingua franca which is the unmarked choice in business talk. Since the conversation between both becomes more personal due to financial problems the client has the accountant switches to Swahili, their common ethnic language, which is then the marked choice. Here, the switch to the Swahili serves a sign of solidarity and group membership. The accountant does that in presenting himself as a person who is, regardless of his status as high educated and prosperous man, helpful with the masses as an "ordinary" person (2003).

However, all these possible outcomes achieved by switching codes have the effect to either increase or decrease the social distance between the speakers within the conversation (Myers-Scotton 1993). Thus, a marked choice which is for example made to express authority or anger has in the end the intention to increase the social distance between the participants. Here, Myers-Scotton explains code switching motivated by psychological factors and in terms of divergence. In contrast to that, a marked choice that is made to reveal one's solidarity aims at the decrease of the social distance between speakers. Thus, code switching can be explained in terms of convergence. At this point, the influence of Howard and Giles becomes obvious who explain language choices in terms of speech accommodation directed in either convergence or divergence.

4.3.2.6 Code switching as an exploratory and neutral choice

According to the third maxim mentioned above code switching can serve as an exploratory choice in cases the speaker is unsure about which is the unmarked choice in a community is. This may occur in situations in which speech exchanges are not conventionalized and where according to Myers –Scotton "there is a clash of norms" (1993: 142). Exploratory code switching may occur on an interpersonal level as well on an intergroup level when societal norms in a community are in a state of fluctuation as a consequence of significant political and historical changes which have led to a change of the language policy (Myers-Scotton 1993). To underline her statement, she refers to the situation in francophone Canada in the 1970ies when a mandate was passed that French replace English in certain contexts. As a result, many people were not certain about what the appropriate language was and thus engaged frequently in code switching. Under those conditions speakers engage in code switching to propose the first language as the appropriate one and then the second one. In doing so the speaker either proposes the rights and obligations set that is associated with this language given the fact that the listener recognizes this intention (1993). Exploratory code switching can further be described as a more or less safe and therefore neutral choice since the speakers employing it try to arrive at a code which seems to be acceptable for all participants of the conversation. Additionally, unmarked code switching can either be regarded as a means to signify neutrality. It is according to Myers-Scotton "the ultimate middle avenue" (1993:147) since speakers avoid tying themselves down to a single rights and obligations set by switching between two languages.

5. Comparison and evaluation of the competing models

5.1 Similarities between the approaches

First of all, all approaches are based on the same premise. The scholars occupied with this topic regard code switching not to be merely random or even a deficit behaviour but rather to be a meaningful feature of bilingual speech. They consider code switching to be an additional resource or skill which is available to bilinguals in order to realize their communicative needs. Even though the approaches offer different arguments in their attempt to explain the motivations for code switching they agree on the fact that bilinguals do not exclusively switch to another language for the reason that they are lacking the appropriate vocabulary of the other language. Thus, all approaches are based on the assumption that next to lacking competence in both languages there are other specific reasons why code switching occurs or that code switching fulfils certain functions for the individual.

According to this, the approaches all have the same intention. They are interested in arriving at the same goal meaning that they want to explore what specific meanings code switching can bear and why bilingual speakers engage in this phenomenon. At this, Fishman may be called an exception. Although he is also interested in the reasons for a particular language choice he analyses this subject with regard to language maintenance and language shift.

Furthermore, most of the approaches take their evidence from naturally occurring everyday conversations which have been observed and recorded between speakers living in bilingual or multilingual communities throughout the world. In other words, most of the approaches rely on the empirical method of fieldwork for their data collection. In most instances, the researchers refer to a specific speech community in which they have conducted their fieldwork. Thus, Peter Auer takes evidence from the German - Italian bilinguals living in Constance, Carol Myers-Scotton conducted her studies mainly in Kenya and John J. Gumperz conducted his fieldwork on code switching in India as well in the United States and Norway. Joshua Fishman observed the Puerto Rican community in Fishman but in addition constructed hypothetical conversations in order to underline his theory on domain- specific language choices.

5.2 The general distinction between macro –level and micro-level perspectives

Within the sociolinguistic study of code switching one can primarily distinguish between macro-level and a micro-level approach which. Both approaches are concerned with the meaning of language but differ in the point where this meaning derives from. Whereas macro-level approaches regard external, societal categories and norms as decisive factors that give meaning to individuals' language choices, micro-level approaches emphasize that the speakers themselves give meaning to their language choices since they attempt to realize particular communicative needs through code switching. In other words, researchers who employ a macro-level perspective regard code switching within more general patterns of language choice in a bilingual or multilingual community whereas those who follow a micro-level approach describe the specific functions of switches within the discourse itself. Briefly speaking, both approaches place a different emphasis at exploring code switching. And whereas both kinds of approaches have contributed immensely to the understanding of code switching, yet they run the risk of applying a too deterministic view.

On the one hand, macro-level approaches run the risk of being too deterministic and abstract by applying a very broad perspective and assigning too much meaning to the roles of social norms without considering the speakers' own intentions. Yet, those who support these approaches regard this kind of abstraction as necessary in order to make broader generalizations about the culture of a speech community.

On the other hand, micro-level perspectives sometimes run the risk of ignoring the role of societal norms at all although it is undisputable that specific patterns of linguistic behaviour cannot be performed without, for instance, the knowledge of situational factors. Nevertheless, it can be said that both perspectives have influenced each other. In his discussion of situational code switching, for instance, Gumperz takes up Fishman viewpoint that topic, interlocutors and the situation are central factors in language choice. Furthermore, other scholars like Myers-Scotton attempt to include macro-level as well as micro-level perspectives into their research of code switching acknowledging that both perspectives have to be considered in order to get to a full understanding of code switching.

5.3. Contributions and limitations to the competing models

5.3.1 Reception and influence of Fishman's domain analysis

In his analysis Joshua Fishman concentrates on determining a variety factors that have an impact on language choice and identified at least three main factors, namely interlocutors, topic and situation which interact with each other in specific domains. Other scholars continued to identify even more factors and domains to which a particular language is assigned to. Yet, the various factors which interact with each other may result in an endless amount of possibilities and situations. The table presented in chapter 4.1.3 gives an idea of some possible constellations and can be extended continuously. However, the listing of several factors is rather descriptive underlying too many exceptions and is therefore inappropriate to explain language choices sufficiently. Being aware of this problem Fishman introduced the concept of domain which is more abstract since it bundles various social situations. However, this view runs the risk of being very deterministic since it seems to be nearly impossible to create an exact one-to-one relationship between a particular activity or domain and an individual language choice. This owes to the fact that there are next to topic, place and situation many other factors that may influence language choice. Thus, a speaker may have a special preference for a particular language. Accordingly, the relation between a domain and a specific language choice is also subject to many exceptions. Therefore, it is nearly impossible to predict which language an individual will choose in a particular situation. Briefly speaking, the correlation between a domain and a language appears to be not strong enough to predict a switch and especially in modern bilingual speech communities many speech events are not strictly tied to one specific language.

5.3.2 The reception and meaning of Gumperz works for ongoing approaches

John J. Gumperz's approach probably belongs to the most cited works in the sociolinguistic literature on code switching. His study on conversational code switching is above all famous for being one of the first approaches to employ micro-level perspective at a time when most of the studies were carried out at a macro-level. Apart from the importance of Gumperz's works for the course of code switching research, there are still some questions which remain unanswered.

First of all, it is Gumperz's basic distinction between 'we'- and 'they codes' which is to some extent arguable. Although Gumperz himself claims that the use of 'we'- and 'they codes' does not actually predict language choices this statement already indicates that it may be even difficult to identify these codes especially in multilingual communities in which various ethnic languages exist next to an official language. With regard to the linguistic diversity given in these communities and the fact that language choice is not strictly tied to specific activities, this distinction between 'we'- and 'they codes' seems to be rather simple to catch the complexity of this issue.

Moreover, the categorization of discourse functions either raises some questions. By listing and briefly explaining the several discourse functions Gumperz remains rather descriptive. Some of the functions such as quotation marking or the insertion of interjections do not reveal much about the speaker's social motivations and what he or she finally achieves through the switch to another language. Nevertheless, Gumperz himself is very aware that his list of discourse functions is rather descriptive and thus only provides the basis for further discussions on the interpretations of these. In other words, he provides the framework in which the interlocutors are left to their own interpretations of conversational code switching as a contextualization cue.

5.3.3 Contrasting Conversation analysis, Speech Accommodation Theory and the Markedness Model

Although these approaches are based on rather different premises they all share the assumption that code switching is one of the most important contextualization cues helping to interpret the speaker's meaning. Thus, especially Auer and Myers-Scotton refer to Gumperz when analysing the functions of code switching.

What distinguishes Peter Auer's conversational analytic approach from Gumperz's as well as Myers-Scotton's is the conviction that context or situation and social meaning are not given beforehand and determined by external, social categories but locally produced within the conversation itself. Speech accommodation theory as well as the markedness model are both based on the assumption that speakers have motives they bring to the conversation whereas conversation analysis stresses that meaning is created within the discourse itself. As a consequence, he is rather concerned with the detailed transcription of surface structures ignoring the role of social norms and values that are associated with languages. Thus, Auer employs a rather deterministic view, in which the practise of conversation analysis is isolated from external factors. However, it is undisputable that social norms influence language behaviour to a certain extent. Thus, it is necessary to take into account what speakers associate with a particular language when they engage in code switching.

The markedness model is unlike the approaches mentioned so far regarded as an attempt to take both micro-level and macro-level aspects into consideration as well as the psychological forces underlying code switching. Taking many perspectives into consideration makes this model relatively complete. The markedness model emphasizes that the participants know which languages are the unmarked and marked choices in a community based on a common, shared experience and that speakers make rational choices intending to achieve the best outcome for them. However, it may be rather debatable that everyday conversations proceed like this and that speech behaviour is always the outcome of conscious calculations.

Speech accommodation theory refers to code switching only in a restricted sense. Revised as communication accommodation theory, it is additionally concerned with the non-verbal aspects of communication. Yet, accommodation theory serves as an convenient tool to describe the motivations underlying language behaviour. Like the markedness model this theory emphasizes the social –psychological motivations within the speaker and assumes that personal experiences are an important factor with regard to language choice. However, speech accommodation theory explains language choices with a particular focus on the addressee. Thus, speakers choose a language depending on either the approval or disapproval of the listener. According to this, the approach runs the risk of loosing sight of the speaker's own goals. Speaker may switch for other, different purposes than for the reason be liked or to be disliked by the addressee.

6. Summary and conclusion

The purpose of this essay was to explore the reasons why bilingual speakers engage in code switching. The theories and models which have been discussed here so far offer a variety of possible answers. Both the society and the individual speaker play a major role in giving meaning to code switching. With regard to societal factors, code switching may occur to situational changes. Concerning the individual speaker, a switch may occur for several reasons. On the one hand, the choice of another language in the same conversation can be performed in order to fulfil several functions for the discourse itself. On the other hand, code switching is employed to express self-identity, group membership and in general certain attitudes towards other persons. However, what is this knowledge of the several functions of code switching and the extensive research on the subject good for?

First of all, the knowledge of the motivations underlying code switching serves as a means to predict a possible switch to another language in a specific situation. Thus, code switching research on the one hand provides information about language use.

Second, code switching is one of many language contact phenomena and therefore the result of daily encounters between speakers of different languages. Thus, code switching research provides on the other hand information about language development.

Third, treating code switching as a relevant research topic and proving that this phenomenon is a social and meaningful behaviour refutes the negative assumption that this language behaviour is deviant and a sign of lacking proficiency in one of the two languages. Thus, code switching research provides above all information on the changing perceptions of bilingualism.

There is no doubt about bilinguals occasionally switching to another language because they do not know the appropriate words in the other language and not every switch may carry social meaning but what has been emphasized by the researchers discussed in this essay is that speakers do not exclusively switch for this reason but further pursuit other purposes by code switching.

Sociolinguistic approaches have contributed to this understanding of code switching as a meaningful resource available to bilingual speakers who use it as an additional means next to other devices such as prosody or gestures in order to realize their communicative needs. In the course of code switching research it has been recognized there has been a tension between macro- and micro-level perspectives and many researchers applied only one of these perspectives. This has finally resulted in a variety of approaches with different explanations. However, there are also approaches which take both perspectives into consideration realising that it is necessary to include social categories as well as individual motivations into the study of code switching.

The sociolinguistic dimension of code switching is one perspective that explores the reasons for code switching. In order to reach a full understanding of code switching it is important to consider the phenomenon not only from a sociolinguistic point of view. Next to the sociolinguistic perspective it is also the grammatical approach to code switching that has contributed immensely to the different perception of code switching as a central feature of bilingual speech.

7. Literature

Apple, René; Muysken, Pieter (1987): *Language contact and bilingualism.* London [u.a.]: Edward Arnold

Auer, Peter (1995): 'The pragmatics of code-switching: A sequential approach. In: Milroy, Lesley; Muysken, Pieter (eds) (1995): *One speaker, two languages. Cross-disciplinary perspectives on code-switching.* Cambridge [u.a.]: Cambridge University Press, pp.115-136.

Auer, Peter (1998): 'Bilingual conversation revisited'. In: Peter Auer (eds) (1998): *Code-Switching in Conversation.* London: Routledge, pp.1-25.

Auer, Peter; Di Luzio, Aldo (eds) (1992): *The contextualization of language.* Amsterdam [u.a.]: John Benjamins Publishing Company

Boztepe, E. (2005 Dec 1): "Issues in Code-Switching: Competing Theories and Models." *Working Papers in TESOL & Applied Linguistics.* <http://journals.tc-library.org/index.php/tesol/article/view/32/37> 2008-09-12

Dimitrijević, Jovana (2004): Code switching: structure and meaning. Series: Linguistics and Literature Vol. 3, No 1, 2004, pp. 37 – 46. University of Melbourne < http://facta.junis.ni.ac.yu/lal/lal2004/lal2004-04.pdf> 2008-09-12

Edel, Kristina (2007): *Strukturen des Bilingualismus, untersucht am Codeswitching Deutsch, Spanisch.* Frankfurt am Main [u.a.]: IKO - Verl. für Interkulturelle Kommunikation

Edwards, John (1994): *Multilingualism.* London [u.a.]: Routledge

Fishman, Joshua (1965):'Who speaks what language to whom and when?'. In: Wei, Li (2000): *The Bilingualism Reader.* London [u.a.]: Routledge, pp. 89-106.

Fishman, Joshua (1999): *Handbook of Language & Ethnicity.* New York [u.a.]: Oxford University Press

Gafaranga, Joseph (2007): 'Code-switching as a conversational strategy'. In: Auer, Peter (eds) (2007): *Handbook of multilingualism and multilingual communication.* Berlin [u.a.]: Mouton de Gruyter, pp.277-310.

Gumperz, John J. (1982): *Discourse strategies.* Cambridge [u.a.]: Cambridge University Press

Haberland, Hartmut (2005): Domains and domain loss. *Department of Language and Culture, University of Roskilde in Denmark.*
<http://www.ruc.dk/cuid/publikationer/publikationer/mobility/>
2008-09-12

Hakuta, Kenji (1999): *Mirror of language. The debate on bilingualism.* New York: Basic Books

Hamers, Josiane F.; Blanc, Michel H.A. (2000): *Bilinguality and Bilingualism.* 2nd. Cambridge: Cambridge University Press

Hoffman, Charlotte (1991): *An introduction to bilingualism.* London [u.a.]: Longman linguistics library . London [u.a.]: Routledge

Li Wei (2000): *The Bilingualism Reader.* London [u.a.]: Routledge, pp. 89-106.

Malmkjær, Kirsten (ed) (2002): *The linguistics encyclopedia.* 2nd London [u.a.]: Routledge

Myers-Scotton, Carol (1993): *Social Motivations for Codeswitching. Evidence from Africa.* New York: Oxford University Press

Myers-Scotton, Carol (2003): *Multiple Voices – An Introduction to Bilingualism.* Malden: Blackwell Publishing

Myers-Scotton, Carol (ed) (1998): Codes and Consequences. Choosing Linguistic Varieties. New York: Oxford University Press

Pfaff, Carol (1998): 'Contacts and conflicts –perspectives from code-switching research'. In: Pütz, Martin (eds) (1998): *Language choices. Conditions, constraints and consequences.* Amsterdam [u.a.]: Benjamins, pp. 341-360.

Redmond, Mark V. (n.d.): Communication Accommodation Theory. Iowa State University.
<http://www.public.iastate.edu/~mredmond/SpAccT.htm>
2008-09-11

Reimann, Anna (2006 Jan 23): Schüler begrüßen Deutsch-Pflicht.
<http://www.spiegel.de/schulspiegel>
2008-09-12

Romaine, Suzanne (1995): *Bilingualism.* 2nd edition. Oxford [u.a.]: Blackwell

Romaine, Suzanne (2000): *Language in society.* 2nd edition. Oxford [u.a.]: Oxford University Press

Thanasoulas, Dimitrios (1999): Accommodation Theory. TEFL.net.
<http://www.tefl.net/esl-articles/accommodation.htm>
2008-09-11